# Twisted

*Honest reflections of a kinky witch*

Ms Quin

Twisted: Honest reflections of a kinky witch

© 2020 Ms Quin

The moral rights of the author have been asserted.

All rights reserved. No part of this publication may be reproduced, distributed, or transmitted in any form or by any means, including photocopying, recording, or other electronic or mechanical methods, without the prior written permission of the publisher, except in the case of brief quotations embodied in critical reviews and certain other non-commercial uses permitted by copyright law. For permission requests, write to the publisher at the email address below.

Content Advisory:
Contains very adult themes, just like life

ISBN 978-1-9163396-4-4

Published by Herbary Books
Caernarfon, Wales

www.herbarybooks.com

# The Toybox

Adoration
1

BABALON I - Summoning Desire's Mistress
5

Blossoms and Thorns
9

Playtime
11

Please, Never a Chore
15

Unbound
17

Note to Self: Let Sleeping Lions Lie
19

Let Me Let Go
21

BABALON II - Serpent Rising
25

Whipcrack Away
29

Tender Wrists
33

Under Your Gaze
35

BABALON III - Making of a Priestess
37

Restrained
41

Learning the Ropes
45

Pretty Sounds
47

The Honey Wiggle
49

Hot Summer Nights...
53

BABLON IV - Babalon Dances
55

Counting the Beat
59

Breathing Space
63

Bound Up in the Moment
67

Fucking Flowers
69

Faery Lover
71

BABALON V - An Offering
75

Painting the Roses Red
77

Unexpected Sanctuary
79

Hidden Marks
81

Epilogue: An Unravelled Rigger's Reflections
85

# *Adoration*

I adore the feel of life,
winter's kiss upon my wrist
twixt glove and cuff
where my armour falters,
summer's slow branding
of audacity to bare
flesh to the world
when I am warm,
soft cloth and softer skin
covering my lover's form
pressed against my own,
tender, passionate, soothing.

I adore the thrum of living
pulsing through my bones
writhing under the surface
driving incessant expression of...

And there I trip.
Tangled in time...
In habits of hiding
and years of punishment
for daring to be
visibly
alive.
But I'm learning
in surrender
to the dance of music and muscle
of beating rhythms
and flowing hands...
In the dare,
and the flash
of being Seen.
In the step-by-step mountain-climb
of reclaiming the forbidden...

This is a love letter.

A song of romance and gratitude for the burning of divinity that courses with every pulse of life through my veins. A prayer offered up, a spell woven from the threads of experience and dreams.

This is a love letter.

A sacrifice of invisibility for the conjuring
of acceptance of the sensuous blessings of
the gods upon each and every one of us.
Life is our birthright. Not mere survival,
but a full-hearted embrace of every moment
within the flesh with which we have been
blessed.

This is a love letter to life. To love.
To desire.

# *BABALON 1 - Summoning Desire's Mistress*

Encircled
by scarlet names
that open and bind.
Eight rays
of Her star.

Her hips sway,
dripping honey,
the earth beneath me
becomes moist
sympathetically.
Long limbs

bound in power
slide through
blood-tinted silks.

Her eyes flash,
dark as stars
watched too long,
and the air around me
grows thick and still.

She sits,
a lioness
coiling itself round
Her prey.
Her fingers soft in my hair,
Her nails sharp.
Blood drips
just a little
to brighten Her veil.
*Dance for me.*

Her voice
lingers in my ears,
her taste on my tongue,
far longer than the rite.

*Dance for me.*

Each night,
Her teeth soft upon my throat.

*Dance for me.*

Each pulse,
Her summons coiling in my spine.

*Dance for me.*

Each mirror,
Her eyes reflecting, meeting mine.

*Dance for me.*

Who could refuse?

They say that only part of communication is in the words, that more of it is in bodies in motion. So many of us are unwilling to be seen dancing, as though our spirits are laid bare in the motion of our flesh and bones and we cannot carry the weight of the longing of our soul's desires being watched.

It is no wonder, when we hide from each other, hide from ourselves, that we become stiff, our bones creak and ache, and we become brittle. It is no wonder that when there is only the armour of stillness we are crushed beneath its weight.

As dust is no way to live. We are spirit-made-flesh, life-in-motion, the divine kissing itself.

Look into Her mirror and let Her show you.

Let your self be seen, even if *only* by your self.

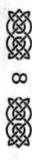

# *Blossoms and Thorns*

A red rose blooms under my skin,
  Marking out my strangeness
    I cannot hide now
      Even if I so desired.

The welts, tiger stripes, declare my self,
  Adoration of life,
    Intensity written on my flesh,
      Where else? Where else?

It worries some, hard to explain
How pain and pleasure become one another.

Or how one could be
unashamed to show that kiss of life.

Crescent moons and ruby blooms
Remind me: I am alive.
In this, my body, my home,
My dance with all that is.

It's a strange thing, a secret hidden, not a thing of shame but a precious jewel kept safe out of sight. Some secrets are kept to protect them, every witch knows this, to keep them safe from those that would break them with misunderstanding and fear. But I've never really been one for staying in the shadows. No one can take my secrets from me because they are carved into my bones. The runes of my longing ache in every sinew and sing in every breath. I weave wishes with my knots and care in each whisper. Life is too short for shame, too fleeting to deny the pleasure and wonder found on the edges of what is taboo. I love life too fiercely to be reckless, but every breath, step, choice is a risk, so why not risk a little misunderstanding to be whole?

# *Playtime*

Can I get out my toys, my dear,
can I get out my toys?
I'm aching to play with my paddle today,
I so love the way it makes noise!

Can I pull out my rope, my dear,
can I pull out my cord?
I'm missing the feel of it, hugging my skin,
keeping me from getting bored.

Can I play with my wand, my dear,
can I please play with my wand?

There's an itch I've really been needing to scratch and it's magic when it's in my hand.

Can you tell me the rules of this game, my dear, can you tell me the rules of this game? I'll follow them all till you nudge me to fall, and when "punished" I'll call out your name!

Can I just be myself, my dear,
can I just be my self?
Let down my hair and dance on to where there's acceptance... it's good for my health!

I've been accused of seriousness, and any jury would convict me. But I choose my playtime with the same reverence as my devotions, and my devotions with the same pleasure as my play. You'd be forgiven for thinking I take myself seriously, but that is only true to a degree, rather; I am seriously committed to delighting in all of life.

When was the last time you played a game? Bought a new toy? Indulged in a fantasy? We are playful creatures, curious and creative. Curious, creative creatures capable of great pleasure... Why not make pleasure a game?

There are few opportunities for play, today.

Between work and sleep and doing what's right and proper we are tired people keeping up appearances. We have given values of good and bad to playfulness and sensations which are simply that. A moment to relax into a game of sensation is a sacred thing. And we have forgotten both the sacred and the sacredness of this serious game of play.

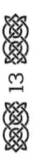

# *Please, Never a Chore*

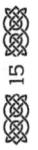

I love to see your eyes glint
to hear your breathing match mine,
I love to know you're enjoying yourself
(so I don't feel I'm stealing your time.)
I adore the catch in your voice when
you know you're the one prompting mine,
your quivering touch when it all gets too much
filled with glee (not a half-suppressed whine.)

I'm turned on by your flash of desire,
rippling passion and longing for more,

so let me know you're enjoying yourself
and, please, that I'm never a chore.

Of all the things *we have* to do, let pleasure not be one of them. Let it be a choice. Let our moments together be chosen, let our joy in each other's company be a gift, let spending time with those we love never be a *chore*.

# *Unbound*

Cords of cotton
Sliding, black, between fingers,
Across soft wrists held outstretched.
Encircling. Once, twice, thrice,
Growing tighter with each turn.
Breath catches,
Pulse speeds,
Restraints releasing all questions
into trust.
Bound, I find myself undone.
Tied to the inescapable moment of now.
Anchored in ecstasy.

I am strange, I know. Something in the way my brain flows allows me to expand. My edges are porous, I am vast. I *feel* the world around me as though I am an ocean rubbing up against it, filling the spaces, slipping into the cracks. I build a cup, a cauldron, a vessel around me with music, with tangible borders, with pressure. *When you touch me, I know where I end and you begin, where I stop and the world expands.*

The caress of cotton cord, of rough jute, or soft silken threads, running across my skin captures my mind and calms my thoughts. The pressure pushes me back into my centre and a web is woven around the etherealness of my self, binding me into my body and this, inescapable, moment.

# Note to Self:
# Let Sleeping Lions Lie

What counts as a need?
Tell me,
which hungers must be fed?

You woke me up
and now I'm ravenous.

For teeth sunk into flesh,
for bruised wrists,
for the burning that consumes,
for that bliss,

and then...
you left.

A lion pacing,
pawing at the floor,
will claw the walls
until there are only doors.

Then,
set loose upon the world,
the lion feasts.

So tell me...
which hungers **must** be fed?

A word to the wise: never try to keep parts of yourself asleep. When they finally become immune to the sweet rocking of the lullaby, or you yourself become too tired to continue the song, they will waken from their hibernation starving, desperate, confused. Either kill them entirely, or give them space to safely be.

But remember, my darlings, you cannot ever outrun your own sweet, hungry, self...

# *Let me Let Go*

Take away my control
tightly wound
holding all the pieces
together
let me dissolve into bliss
for once
in your care

A wild goddess spins
just out of reach
I can't break these chains alone
can't reach her from where I'm locked

I don't know how.

But you might.

Wrap me in your ropes,
pin me
with leather
with flesh
mark my edges with violet
pain
hold me down
and let me
let
go
screaming

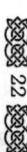

hold me
so I don't have to hold myself
together
let me
writhe
into dissolution
into flames
pulsing
burning
let me
let
go

before I drown in the flood
dammed too long.

Fuck me senseless
because sense is
what got me
into this mess.

I'm such a control freak. A hold-your-life-together-through-sheer-force-of-will monster of a person. A mentally-take-everything-apart-piece-by-piece-to-make-sure-it-all-matches-the-plan overthinker. I hold so tightly, so hard, that I don't know how to let go.

*I didn't know how to let go.*

There's a moment when you find yourself crossing a threshold, passing a point into the unknown, where you have to place your trust in others. You can learn all you like about safety, vet the people around you, take precautions, think it through and shape the space, but at a certain point you just have to let them hold you.

You have to let go.

Let go of what you've learned, how you've been taught to respond, what you think you know. What is present now? What is truly harmful? What is truly desired? What is true?

Let go of the patterns, of the lies, of the illusions.

Let go of sensible.

Fall into True.

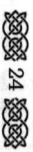

# BABALON II - Serpent Rising

Inside, the beast paces,
lion's paws insistent on the
concrete of the pit.

No.

Less contained than that.

Welling up,
a flame that consumes,
rapturous.

The serpent rising
is not so much a smooth thing
as a flood.

An uncoiling of oceans
unravelling

be my undoing

wyrm,
deeper,
bathing underground
in the cavernous lakes
of lust
lapping at the edges
of me

until
undammed
we overflow, erupting
into life.

In answer to the call of desire, She draws near. The vibrancy of life shimmering within all possibility, memories of the stars that we were lighting our way, lighting Her way within us.

Her's is a love song. The melody of the night sky rippling over pounding bass that beats in our blood. Can you hear it?

Her's is a love song, flashes of sweet laughter as we fumble along in our heartfelt longing to be good enough for the blessing that drips from her lips...

Hoping we'll be the chosen ones.

Forgetting... we've always been the chosen ones.

# *Whipcrack Away*

Pick me! Pick me!
I wanna try!
Then out come the targets
and inside I'm shy.
Dangling teddies
all in a row
I'm handed the whip
so now it's my go...
Remember to breathe,
flow and take aim...
It cracked! I'm winning!
Let's try it again!

Cue madly flailing
as adrenaline spreads
and my early success
goes straight to my head.
Everyone's watching,
how could they not?
My heart's all a-flutter,
both cheeks getting hot.

Feet replanted firmly
in my bright yellow boots,
with a gentle reminder
I feel for my roots...
With a roll of the whip
and a flick of the wrist
I tap Tigger not my target,
but at least he still twists!

In time, seems forever,
I'm relieved of my turn,
and beaming with pride
convinced whipping I'll learn.
I'll have to save up first,
and study it well,
but for now, teddy-cuddles,
'cause Tigger did swell!

There's a level of skill required in anything that walks the edge.

That first moment of picking up a whip - a weapon - in front of a crowd no less. Of feeling it's serpentine weight in my fingers, seeing the targets dangling before me. I'm used to an audience, but that's not why I'm here. Like loosing a bow, there is a focus in throwing a whip, a deep breathing Flow and a meditative singlemindedness. There's a thrill in success, and a learning curve in balancing that thrill with the calm that gives space for it to happen again.

Part of the skill is in finding that calm. That focus. That presence.

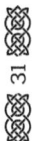

Finding my feet in the moment, to meet possibility head on.

# *Tender Wrists*

Tenderness
gets under my skin
in the best way.
Bruises
too deep to see;
reminders
inspiring aftershocks
of rippling bliss
for days...

Ever wished for a memento of a wonderful night?

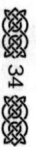

# *Under your Gaze*

I am
tangled in your threads,
watched,
intently.
Becoming a work of art, no,
a canvas
for your weaving.
A web wound,
round,
binding me
to your will.
You find your power,

I see it rise from the soft, dark, earth,
and I surrender.
My mind fades under your gaze.

I am taken
with you.

Ariadne spun the thread that led the hero from the maze and thus became the spider goddess, spinning fates and futures and far reaching connections. Connection. Between people. That meeting of two beings in roles both clearly defined and so mutable, meldable. In your ropes I become a work of art, beauty underlined by twists of the web which show your power in control, my power in surrender, our trust in each other.

# BABALON III - Making of a Priestess

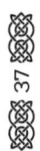

Sometimes a Goddess comes.
Not even sometimes,
no.
Yes,
always.
In every breath,
every dance-step,
every lick,
every kiss.

*All acts of love and pleasure are my rituals.*

All She asks for
is your life.
Each moment,
fully lived.

*All acts of love and pleasure.*

The stars spin
in Her eyes
in Her stride
in the tips of every nerve
caressed by Her breath
on the wind.

*All acts of love and pleasure.*

Always, the Goddess cums.
All time
one time
one moment of Creation
of Orgasmic
bliss.

*All acts are love and pleasure.*

From Her pleasure, existence was born. The Word was not a dry whisper but a cry of delight, a deepfelt roaring of longing for the dance of love. The mother of all existence has no shame in Her desire, She pulsates

with it through every second of eternity,
sharing it freely with all who have hearts to
beat in time with Her's.

What greater blessing could there be than
this? Than living? Than life in all its sensuous,
messy, sticky, blissful, desiring dance?

# *Restrained*

Won't it get sticky?
I wonder aloud,
I'm told it gets slick
by the grinning crowd.
I return with my prize
gingerly won
with some trepidation
as he helps slide it on.
The rubber is smooth
against my bare skin
a gentle caress,
rising wonder within...

Zip riding higher
and straps swiftly tugged
with arms pinned around me
to the pole I am led.
There on the dancefloor
straightjacket's embrace,
couldn't leave if I wished to
held in my place.
The chatter receding
constrained by the feel
of my edges defined
and a warmth oh so real...
Restlessness tamed
as attention is drawn
to this moment and movement
and the pull on each arm,
My breathing grows heavy
I sink into my core
heavy and hot and
longing for more.
I'm alive, all electric,
and hungry for touch
all expansion condensed;
it's almost too much.
I shudder, he chuckles,
bringing a smile.
I guess a rubber straightjacket
brings me home for a while.

Sometimes the strangest things help the world make sense.

# Learning the Ropes

Black cotton cutting
into translucent skin, soft
under sliding hands.

Laughter, puzzlement,
between soft gasps of heaven
as knots are learned.

Tension, pulling down,
pinning me to the table.
He admires his work.

Strange how that moment
of enforced surrender is
when I'm most alive.

There's a part of me that longs for this, longs to be able to hand over the reins, let the rules be set by someone else for once (I'd never submit to just any rules though, they must be fair, and kind, and bounded by trust... but I digress). But I do not place my trust in just anyone. For someone else to hold my reins I must trust that they are better at control as I am, or at least as good. I trust myself to hold my edges, but who else would ever, could ever, be strong enough? I trust myself to follow the compass that guides me, but who else would ever, could ever, prove themselves to hold to it as well as I?

So I play. For a moment, physically held, I feel my soul surrender.

# *Pretty Sounds*

*"You make such pretty sounds."*
I hear you say
as you
draw pleasure along my spine
with your nails.

And I cannot help it.

I chose to let go
to place myself
in your care
and not hold back.

And now I cannot stop,
I do not even want to.

After,
I worry about the judgement.
Pleasure is a private thing,
not for a club,
not for sharing where
strangers can hear.
The sounds of bliss
must be quieted...
How old stories linger...

But for you,
for me,
I won't hold back.

The universe is a song, each of us breathes our own note in the melody of the world for as long as we are here. It takes a confidence so often beaten out of us (hopefully metaphorically) to let our voices be heard. Perhaps losing ourselves in the moment, giving our voices over as a gift to those that are meeting us in the tune we long to play, is where that confidence can be beaten back into us (possibly literally...).

# *The Honey Wiggle*

Hard here to hide
               in bright yellow stripes
with boppers that bounce
               and a corset that's tight
But I'm hiding my face
               and I'm closing my eyes
as the moment I'm in
               is just the right size.
If I'd looked up
               seen the people stood round,
Eight he now tells me,
               well that's quite a crowd,

I'd have been thinking
        of what they must see,
not feeling delight
        at just being a bee,
with a sting in my tail
        and invisible wings,
all my attention
        on my Cap'n's swings.
Completely surrendered
        to this final Now...
Though next time,
        perhaps,
               I'll play to the crowd...

*Perhaps I really am an exhibitionist...*

Nail, meet head.

I feel like such a private person. Casual nakedness is not my game, sharing nudes holds no intrigue. If I undress for you I want to be savoured, I want to feel your skin against mine, those edges of two worlds meeting, that connection as electricity flows from flesh to flesh...

But I am a performer. I adore the adoration of the crowd, I crave the attention, the light. I love to make an impression, to be remembered fondly.

*What is remembered, lives.*

But it wars within me. Some moments, I need to just keep, just for me, just between us. To turn that gaze outwards into the glamour would be to move from how it feels to *be* into how it feels to *appear*. But sometimes, I simply *am* in the spotlight. Being and being seen, all at once. At that crossroads I *shine*.

# *Hot Summer Nights...*

"I forget that you're an inlander."
I hear you say as I
gaze
longingly at the waves
the sand,
the sun.
And you indulge me,
oh, you indulge me...
My leash undone
foam soaks my thighs
and
there are dolphins

and
moonlit fun
and
oh holy fuck
I think the
whole
town
just heard me...

Ehem.

*Sometimes it really is just about sex.*

# *BABALON IV -*
# *Babalon Dances*

Babalon dances
her glory rising,
veils turning stars
in the darkness,
supernovas.

The Always-Never-Chained, She is.
The Mistress of Desire.
Rider of the Beast
and Sacred Whore.

BABALON.

Scarlet Goddess,
in
velvet and furs,
silk and leather;
the skins of Her enemies
cut
by Her own blades.

BABALON.

Queen of Heaven.
Power of the Deep.
I know your name
and it is LUST.

BABALON.

She has such a bad reputation, how could she not? A powerful being drenched in all those things civilisation sweeps under the carpet.

A Goddess of sex and war and blood? She dances in each of us, under the veneer of *normal*, in the wishes for freedom, the rising of passion, the flashes of fury when we are disrespected.

To the forces of Order, She looks like a demon.

And wouldn't you come up swinging if
you'd been continually stuffed in a box?

Don't you *want* to come out swinging?

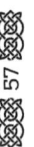

# *Counting the Beat*

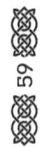

Squirming under the sting,
World wiped out
in kinetic contact.

And...
Breathe...
Five.

Foot thumpingly
deliciously
overwhelming.

And...
Breathe...
Six.

Thoughts return to the room,
after each beat,
choosing to go on.

And...
Breathe...
Seven.

Forced to stay present
slipping away,
riding pain...

And...
Breathe...
Eight.

An exercise in letting go,
determination,
trust.

And...
Breathe...

Dissolution.
Momentary, total, surrender.

And...
Nine.

It seems
I like this game…

*Consent.* Choosing each and every moment to stay, to continue, to endure and enjoy and entice more… Learning that this is a choice means learning that you can walk away. Finding your strength. It means learning to say no, and learning to say yes, *thank you*, *more*. To speak and act your truth, in every moment of your life.

# *Breathing Space*

Back at the hotel
blank white sheets
on which to,
laughing,
lay
blossoming bruises
tenderly

a moment of quiet
deep
in
the night

in between
strikes

the pauses
for breath
between
beats
between
stars
of pain
between
Yes
and Wait...
between
the striking of oak
and sharp edges
on soft places

Gasping,
yelping,
indignation
echoes
round the dungeon...
and
in between...

Between the longing
and the pain...

The still
white
space...

Kink creates such intense experiences you'd think the moments in between would feel grey in comparison, but no. The space between the adventures take on a special quality. The mind has learned to *be* in the moment and so it continues. Worries released, tension banished, safety found. It casts an enchantment on life as a whole. The strength of the beautiful darkness permeates the days that fall between in an embodiment of flesh and spirit and the lessons learned. Endurance, euphoria, patience, trust, delight. The peaceful bliss of being alive.
      Tight.

# *Bound Up in the Moment*

Let your breath
... ease ...
Held;
jute wrapped close.
Safe.
Feel the edges
of your self
defined.
Mustn't fight it
just listen to your body
and
learn to

... Be ...
Bound.

Flip the longing on its head. There's a fight in the game - *I will not be stopped.* Untamed, relentless. A storm on the horizon. Who wants to be in a teacup? The china shatters and a sound has never been sweeter. Captured and bound - a struggle. Wrestling against bonds that can be felt is so much more satisfying than pressing against the intangible. The restraints become manifest our limits wrought in iron and leather and chain and rope pinning limbs and restricting breath and giving something anything everything to fight against when the whole world is just too big to encompass and hold and it overwhelms and and and

slowly, the fight subsides.

Acceptance, or defeat.

With it; peace.

# *Fucking Flowers*

Whichever way the wind blows
in a valley in the spring,
you're getting pollinated.
To be precise;
fucked by flowers.

I fall in love at every scented petal
dog roses growing wild
seduce me
as I wander the fields,
breathing in their...
...blessings,

until paroxysms pulse through
my flesh
in a moment of release.

Does hayfever make one an ecosexual?

*Sometimes... it's **all** about sex.*

# *Faery Lover*

Slipping my skin
I drift
down

past alder roots
and turning worms
awaiting Persephone.

Below
the dark forest waits.
A glade with roses

bathed in starlight,
it gives to me.

Here
my silver-tongued lover
clothed in green
takes my hand
and leads me to the softest bed
of moss
and thorns grow over my limbs
biting.
Blood drips,
my gift to the soil,
to the blooms.

Petals open
nectar flows
tongues taste deeply
and we begin to fly.

When dawn comes
- all too soon -
I return to my skin,
my lover's song
of pleasure
still in my ears.

If you think this is all a fantasy you've never lain in dappled starlight as the wind gently raises the tiny hairs across your flesh, or dipped your toes in cool running water and felt the erotic power of the world around us, or bathed in sunlight and sweat as you move your body to the music which demands that you open your heart and celebrate all that is possible in this moment.

If you think this is all a fantasy, you're right, and oh so wrong.

# *BABALON V -*
# *An Offering*

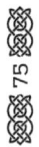

Silk sliding,
slipping, cross skin,
sharp and cool and soothing on scratches,
dripping pomegranate red.

Bronze shimmers,
catching sweetness,
freely given sacrifice of sacred scars,
mapping on theurgy's bed

deep guidance,
ancient star-song,

lighthouses along the shore of magic's
waves
better longing than dead.

Heavy curtains,
hiding wishes,
hiding power vulnerable and wild,
keeping safe in silent dread.
Better longing, now, than dead.

There's a risk in everything we do. Heartbreak lurks round every corner, every wish reached for is a chance that all our dreams will burn. Every time we walk away from what we have for what could be... we could end up with nothing. Or everything we ever imagined.

Where there's fear, there's power.

In the end we all become nothing, why let trepidation keep us smaller than we could be before then? Why be walking-dead when we could *live*?

# *Painting the Roses Red*

Thorns bite
deep
painting my wrists
scarlet.

Mustn't struggle.
Each movement,
fresh wet warm dripping
from fingertips.

Beauty of blossoms,
Once white,

below my palms.

I am entranced
held by love
cut by the same
that keeps me pinned.

Intoxicated
by the thrill;
Too easily caught.

Now I daren't move
as, if they bite much more,
I'll wash the blooms away.

Bravado is not the same as expansion...

Did you know a heart can literally break?
Our body-mind is all one, we are spirit
walking, and those feelings are as powerful
as any physical pain. The bite of loss, the
nausea of uncertainty, the gut-punch of
grief. And, drowning in emotion coursing
through the body, we tighten the floodgates
of our lips just in case it would drown our
lover too.

# *Unexpected Sanctuary*

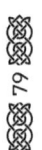

A sanctuary of
sharp
nails
marking soft flesh
to remind me
I am held, known, loved.
How did you know
that would help?
I guess you've been in this place before.
The marks linger
crescent moons
just briefly.

A gentle pain, clear sensation to anchor
the thoughts in a swirl of panic. Nails
pressed hard into my palm bring me back.
Little things littered through my life are
tiny lanterns lighting the way towards my
inclinations. So many things hurt that not
all pain means danger. Sometimes, the right
pain, means sanctuary... and knowing the
difference, choosing carefully, is where the
healing begins.

# *Hidden Marks*

Sometimes I catch my shirt
on the marks you've left behind the night
before
and I smile.
A secret smile,
understood by only me
though I'm not the only one who knows it
from the inside.

Sometimes I see the darkness
under my skin

and I am carried back into the moment
where only you and I have been.

Sometimes I understand
why these signs are Not Allowed out there,
when they are doorways to a space all our own.

When they whisper of places
outside the reach of control,
when they hint to those that might see
that more is possible.

And sometimes...
Most times, I'm sure you understand...
...I keep these maps just for me.

It's a strange thing, to carry secret jewels through life, blossoms and dark maps of memories of where I've been. The marks fade, and are incidental to start with, but while I bear them they are delicious reminders of tenderness and care, of connection and sanctuary, of playfulness and peace.

In the challenges we choose for ourselves we face Her blade, point to our heart, demanding to know why we deserve to step forward into power. Am I pure of intention? Can I trust the twists and turns ahead?

Do I place myself in Her care, armed with
as much knowledge as can be gleaned before
action turns it into wisdom?

On this meandering path lit by the starlight
of love and pleasure, magic and choice,
I have unravelled myself to find my way
back to where I've always been drawn to and
here, in the ropes and the rubber, the sensation
and the laughter, the connection and the
calm hard-won through focus, flow, surrender,
here I find myself weaving myself together
again, in the arms of the Goddess, in the
arms of Love.

# Epilogue

# *An Unravelled Rigger's Reflections*

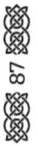

My mind has unravelled,
threads unstrung,
with the weavings of my life
where dreams once hung.

Sinking further and deeper
into who I am
finding fire in my flesh
and knowledge like sand...

Tattered and rebuilding
with embers left behind

from the wildfire burning,
but change isn't kind.

I'm aching and I'm longing
as my old skins fall
stepping closer to my Northern Star
I heed Her call...

The path ahead is golden
moonlight on the sea,
though it ripples and it wavers
it is clear enough to me.

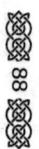

My mind has unravelled,
threads unstrung,
with the weavings of my life
where dreams once hung.
Yet with fingers deftly twisting,
turning, spinning threads unspun,
a new web of wyrd is woven,
brighter dreams begun...

# WITH A LOVE FOR BOOKS

With a large range of imprints, from herbal medicine, self-sufficiency, physical and mental wellbeing, food, memoirs and many more, Herbary Books is shaped by the passion for writing and bringing innovative ideas close to our readers.

All our authors put their hearts into their books and as publishers we just lend a helping hand to bring their creation to life.

Thank you to our authors and to you, dear reader.

---

Discover and purchase all our books on
**WWW.HERBARYBOOKS.COM**

www.ingramcontent.com/pod-product-compliance
Lightning Source LLC
Chambersburg PA
CBHW071749080526
44588CB00013B/2192